Testimonials

"Your presentation in America was brilliant. You had all
- who were directors of BNI from all over the world - in the palm of
your hand. It was engaging, witty, impactful and - most of all - had
brilliant content. I was really pleased to have been in the room, and I
know that view was shared by everyone I spoke to afterwards."

2nd June 2006
Andy Bounds, author of 'The Jelly Effect'

"Iain was an inspirational leader. He devoted himself wholeheartedly
to encouraging all BNI members and brought innovation and
enthusiasm to the organisation. He always looked to develop his own
skills whilst developing the skills of others. He gave unstintingly of
his time and stuck with his vision of assisting others."

April 10, 2007
Jo Middlemiss, Owner, Dreamzwork

"I first met Iain in 2003 at a BNI conference in the UK. He is easy to
get to know and follows all the principals of good networking. Since
that time we have worked successfully together on both sides of the
world. Iain is a good friend and an excellent strategic alliance."

September 29, 2007
Jack Fraenkel, Owner, Motivatories Pty Ltd

"I would like to take this opportunity to thank you for the business
advice and guidance you have given to Full Circle Graphics, both
through your seminars and on a one-to-one basis. Your 'blunt
honesty' has hit home in a number of areas within our business and
the changes that this has resulted in has made vast improvements
to our business moving forward in a more structured and positive
manner and most importantly to our bottom line."

24th April 2009
David Tod, Partner, Full Circle Graphics LLP

Life, Business
& Speedboats

Iain Whyte

bigmantalking.com

This book is dedicated to my partner Val and my two beautiful daughters Morag and Heather. To Val, for putting up with me and supporting me at all times no matter how mad my ideas have been, and to my two girls for putting even the craziest, most frustrating day into perspective.

I also thank Ron Hain for giving me the opportunities he did before he was taken from us all too early in life. Likewise I thank Chris Norman, a constant source of fun, laughter and ideas. He also was lost to us far too soon. I miss them both and hope they discover not only what they both meant to me but also how they influenced this book and my life. God Bless them both.

Foreword

This book owes its existence to BNI (Business Network International), the largest referral organisation in the world today. As a member and Director I have had the privilege of travelling the globe and meeting business people worldwide. To all the members and Directors of BNI, I owe so much, and none more so than Dr Ivan Misner, BNI's Founder and Chairman. Ivan has been an inspiration, always there with a helpful word and a generous dose of encouragement. In particular, this book has been helped into life by Ivan's Author Mentee scheme which he willingly shares with every BNI Director who wishes to participate.

I hope that you learn at least One Big Thing from this book, whatever that Thing might be. In fact, as a business person you will probably have heard most of the content before. But just ask yourself this: when was the last time you acted on it? All too often, we know what to do but fail to do it in case it doesn't work. Trust me, it will. Regular actions achieve results. It's our job to control our actions – so keep taking action and the results will simply happen.

Introduction

Congratulations on your investment! In this book, I'll be covering business issues from administrators to zoning, spiders to logs, and sun-kissed beaches to icebergs.

Not what you expected? Well, in writing this I'm assuming that you want to run a business... and that you'd prefer not to be stuck in a job in which you're both 24/7 employer and 24/7 employee.

Now, please grab your pen or pencil and a highlighter. As you work through the book, highlight the key points and jot down any ideas as soon as they occur to you. Otherwise, one slight distraction and you'll lose that great idea you just had. Believe me, I know. And stomping around trying to remember just what it was doesn't work. It does mean you get tetchy and your blood pressure skyrockets. Better to go and do cartwheels.

Alternatively, just jot down your ideas as they occur to you.

I hope you'll continue thinking about the issues raised here as you go about your daily business or take the dog for a walk. So if you can, get into the habit of carrying around a notebook and pen, dictaphone or maybe a divers' writing board (in case an idea pops up while you're swimming. There's nothing like being prepared.).

Confidence & Referrals

*… or how to quickly instil confidence in people so they'll want to help **you** take **your** business forward.*

Here's a fundamental question every business owner should answer: 'What's the purpose of your business?' Most will reply, 'To acquire and keep profitable clients.' In other words, **you're in business to make profits**. Even if you run a charity, you've got to make more money than you spend.

But what have referrals and confidence got to do with each other? A lot, in fact. If people lack confidence in you, they won't tell other people about you (unless they're telling them to stay away from your business, and you really don't want that).

Let's take a quick look at why people might not have confidence in you.

- Someone's been telling bad stories about you (and if the stories aren't true it's time to sue).

- They weren't really sure what they wanted and even after speaking to you they're still unsure.

- Your goods or services are shoddy.

- You haven't delivered on time.

- You're charging more than you said you would.

- They lack confidence in themselves or their decisions. Or maybe things are bad in their life right now and they're suppressing the thoughts… and they're projecting their insecurities or anger onto you.

• You lack confidence in yourself / your service / your product. And it shows.

Confidence can be a strange and nebulous thing. But you can gain confidence in yourself and in what you offer to others. By building your own confidence, you can build your prospects' and clients' confidence in you.

And if people have confidence in you they'll:

• buy from you.

• pass your name on to other people.

Brilliant! So confidence can equal referrals. And *if you act on them promptly*, referrals are the best kind of business you can get.

Confidence = Referrals = £££s for you

Let's recap: people who are referred to you are more likely to use your products or services than those who come across you by chance.

So referrals are critical to the future success of your business.

People I coach often say at this point, 'Yeah, but…':

- 'Yebbut I don't know enough people who have the right contacts.'

- 'Yebbut I'm shy.'

- 'Yebbut they'll think I'm rude to ask.'

- 'Yebbut what happens if they don't like my product?'

- 'Yebbut, Yebbut, Yebbut, Yebbut…'

In fact, people often think that it's really hard to find others who'll refer work to them regularly.

But is it? Maybe the ideal referral source for you is nearer than you think…

However, before I show you that, I'd better dispel those Yebbuts I quoted above!

'Yebbut I don't know enough people who have the right contacts'

1. How do you know that?

2. If you're sure, then do something about it.

I have a friend who loves networking. She discovers a lot about her contacts by asking the right questions, listening to them, and remembering what they've said or writing it down. She also finds out about who her contacts know and who their contacts are?

When she needed to ask someone about RSS[1] feeds, for example, she asked a few friends. Since building websites wasn't really their thing they didn't know what she was talking about, but one of the group gave her the name of someone who *could* help.

This friend asks a lot of people about a lot of things. She has enough self-confidence that she's not afraid of people knowing she doesn't have all the answers. And she realises that people like to **help** rather than laugh at her ignorance (or what I like to call 'temporary un-knowledge'. It sounds kinder).

It's actually very easy to find people to ask. Just join networking groups, then learn to mingle, ask and listen. The groups might meet in person (like BNI, the Chamber of Commerce and training conferences, for example), or they might be cybergroups (individuals communicating through webinars and online forums, for example). None round your way? Start one up.

'Yebbut, I'm shy'

Lots of people are – and often you wouldn't know it to look at them. You can go on courses to help you overcome shyness, get help to conquer it (counselling, CBT[4], TFT[3], NLP[2],etc.), and actually attend networking events. It's amazing how easy networking can be: just ask people about themselves, their businesses and their needs. And show you're listening. People will really warm to you.

[1] *RSS: Rich Site Summary*
[2] *NLP: Neuro-Linguistic Programming*
[3] *TFT: Thought Field Therapy*
[4] *CBT: Cognitive Behavioural Therapy*

Ask what you can do to help the person you're talking to. You'll find when you're helping someone towards a solution, the words flow more easily and you begin to smile without trying.

Here's a golden rule: don't cling to the first person who speaks to you! Ask them (for example) if they know someone who can help you find a good printer for your stationery. If they do, ask them to introduce you.

Ask people for their business cards, and offer yours in return. Make sure that your cards clearly show the benefits you offer. Your new acquaintances may well pass them on saying, 'I don't really know that much about Julie's product, but she seems very genuine: why don't you give her a call?'

'Yebbut, they'll think I'm rude to ask'

Um, who says? It wouldn't occur to most folks and they'll usually be happy to help. Just make sure they understand what you're asking of them by being specific (more on that later).

'Yebbut, what happens if they don't like my product?'

Depends why! If your product is shoddy, then you have no right anyway to be putting someone in an awkward position. Change your product and then ask again.

Sometimes it's not so much that someone dislikes your product, it's simply that they don't like that product in general – or don't need it at that time. Me, I don't like golf, so I'm not going to be interested in your golf stuff. However, just because someone doesn't like or need your product doesn't mean they won't pass your name on. So while I might not like golf, I do know plenty of avid golfers. And if your state-of-the-art new club will swipe 16 strokes off their total, then I'll definitely tell them about you.

'Yebbut, Yebbut, Yebbut, Yebbut, ...'

Maybe you're just a 'glass half-empty' person, or maybe you're just in the wrong business...

Work out whether you're in your particular business because you want to be, or because you feel you should be, or because someone else wants you to be. Find your passion and work with that. If it's just one part of your business that bothers you (for me, it's book-keeping and filing), then outsource that part.

So, back to where we left off: the bit where I was saying that the ideal referral source for you is nearer than you think...

Target Market Commonality

Ever heard that phrase, 'Market Commonality' (MC)? Well, target it!

What's MC? Basically, groups of business people who share the same types of clients can join forces, swap their clients easily, form a common bond and hit their targets in the best possible way. Become part of that force!

For instance, you might be a web designer. Get together with graphic designers and copywriters so you can target start-up businesses, those who want to move into online sales, or others whose web presence is currently weak, dodgy or positively gruesome.

If you're a solicitor wanting to talk to non-English nationals who are setting up businesses in the UK, you might want to know an accountant, someone who writes in plain English, a printer, a translator, and so on.

Why would you look for an MC group (or groups)? The main benefits are that as you build up trust among your group members, you can:

• get more business.

• feel more confident about yourself.

• ask for and receive more referrals.

• feel a lot less lonely.

Take the time here to identify your MC group or the types of people you'd like to approach and get to know.

You could use a table like this one:

Type of prospect I want to target New businesses (small ones)		Where I might find them Chamber of Commerce; New biz gvt schemes; biz forums		
MC Person	**Website**	**Email**	**Tel.**	**Comments**
Brian Callam	www.bclawyer.com	brian@bclawyer.com	01222 123456	Solicitor; does free terms & conditions for new businesses

Type of prospect I want to target		Where I might find them		
MC Person	Website	Email	Tel.	Comments

So, we've now seen that because we have a lot of target market commonality with a great many people, there are many people who are potentially good referrers for our businesses.

However, to maximise the number of referrals we get and cause an energy shift in our 'client conveyor belt', it's absolutely critical that we **target, approach, cultivate and execute the right relationships in the right way.**

This is where 'The Five Fundamentals of Referrals' come in.

The 'Five Fundamentals of Referrals'

We've explored how confidence and referrals go hand in hand. Now we'll look at five main concepts in more depth. We'll look at how to motivate by giving; how to instil confidence in others; how to educate others as to what you want; how to keep disciplined; and how to find the right referral partners.

- ○ Motivate through 'Givers Gain'.

- ○ Instil confidence.

- ○ Educate others on who and how.

- ○ Stay disciplined.

- ○ Find the right referral partners.

Motivate through 'Givers Gain'

I run BNI Scotland South & East. As in all BNI 'chapters' (groups), we open every meeting by reminding people that 'givers gain' … and with good reason. It's one of the most powerful tenets of business. If you're just in business with a view to making profits and blow all else, then you run the risk of having a lonely time – and you'll be much less likely to get referrals.

It's a widely held belief that people manifest their thoughts and feelings – call it karma, putting out the vibes, the Law of Attraction – whatever. It all amounts to the same thing. If you're good to people, you'll benefit. Maybe not immediately, but sometime, when you need it, it'll come back to you.

For instance, one business friend of mine was always there to help others. She didn't do it with reward in mind; she just likes people and enjoys sharing her knowledge. At one meeting she stood up to speak about her business (more on how to talk about your business later), and she hesitated. People began to smile as she could usually be relied on to do something humorous, and then realised she was quite upset.

She explained her major client had just pulled out without any warning: 'Yes, I know, I shouldn't have relied so much on having work from just one source, but the owner was a good friend. I'd have expected some notice! But anyway, I don't have enough work at all. I need help, please.'

The group rallied around her, some offering support, a couple offering loans, and several phoning through with referrals that week. Her work level was soon back on track… as was her self confidence.

Instil confidence

We've established that to generate referrals you need confidence.

You must have confidence in your service or product and you should be seen to have confidence. Others need to share that confidence and they must know that your promises will be kept. When they feel you are offering a sound service, they may pass your name on. I say 'may' because nothing is guaranteed. It helps if they like you and if they know who/what you're looking for (more about that later too).

So how can you help instil confidence within yourself and others? We'll start with you, and then look at how you can spread the 'message'. I'm assuming here you're running your own business, or maybe working on a commission basis for someone else.

First, you must believe in your product or service. Would you buy it? If not, why not? Maybe it's because you have no need of it right now: in that case would you buy it for a member of your family or a close friend? Can you honestly say that your product is better than someone else's? If you can't, do you make up for the shortfall by offering it at a reduced rate to a different set of buyers? If you are trying to get away with promoting something as better than it is, it'll show.

For those who work on commission it really, really helps to believe that what you're selling will benefit your potential buyers. If you don't, get out now! You have plenty of transferable skills, and many businesses require good sales people.

When people ask you about your product or service, don't launch into a feature-laden explanation, and don't go on about your business ('We were established in 1994, blah, drone, blah') unless they specifically ask. Instead, talk enthusiastically about how your product has helped your clients or customers. Find out why the enquirer has bothered to ask you, and give your answer in a way that draws their situation (or their friend's) into your reply.

For example: Can I ask why you're interested in my Super-Duper Triac drill set? Oh, you need some shelves up? No? Oh, your neighbour does, and is looking for something easy to use. Well, really she doesn't need a drill per se – she needs holes in the wall! Our drill set is rechargeable and lightweight, with a head that turns. It has a mounted light on it too, so she can get into awkward corners, and not worry about cupboards being unlit, or about finding an extension cable, and the holes she wants will appear like magic ...' (And so on – I think you'll have got the picture.)

You can also display your confidence by advertising, dealing politely and efficiently with complaints and returns, and by giving guarantees.

If you consistently advertise your product or service, people will assume that (a) you believe in it, and (b) it must be good and profitable otherwise you wouldn't keep advertising, and (c) they'll feel comfortable because they recognise your name and know you're not a fly-by-night.

Be up-front too about how you would deal with an unsure prospect or an unhappy customer. If you're seen to have a good guarantee and a non-fussy returns policy, people will have more confidence in referring you to others. If you fight your corner over something that others perceive as a minor issue (even if you are convinced you're in the right), negative word will spread.

Unless it's really worth fighting over, be as gracious as possible. You can even go a bit further: 'I'm sorry this wasn't what you needed. Please accept a refund and this bouquet of flowers for your trouble.' That sort of word will travel too ☺.

The last bit of confidence comes in people knowing exactly what your products or services offer, and who they need to talk to about you. Let them know. Which leads us nicely onto…

Educate who and how

Be specific, give examples, tell stories, and repeat.

And, of course, find people to educate, especially those who understand business and how to find prospects for you. What I'm saying is, just chatting at a social event may get you some referrals, but belonging to business groups can get you a whole lot more.

I'll use BNI as the example here, but there are plenty of business groups that give you a chance to 'pitch your wares' either within a formal structure or as you circulate and chat with other members.

What happens is, you get a period of time to promote your offer and to ask for the referrals or introductions you want. Some people refer to your speech as an 'elevator pitch'. The premise here is that you're in an elevator with a stranger (who might of course be able to help you) and you've got until you get to the top floor to impress them and explain what you want.

So, what components do you need in your pitch? Let's say you're allowed 60 seconds. In that time:

Let's take that bit by bit: (Points expanded on page 30.)

- Greet everybody and state your name and your business name.
- Give your tag line/USP.
- Grab attention with a strong headline.
- Tell a story or say what you do.
- Describe the sort of referrals you are looking for.
- Give your name, name of your business and tag line.

First, here's a reminder of where we've got up to in this section:

✓ Motivate through 'Givers Gain'.

✓ Instil confidence.

✓ Educate others on who and how.

We've covered these points so far

○ Stay disciplined.

○ Find the right referral partners.

These two are also essential parts to your business-building plot

---

Stay disciplined

This section is short, but no less important. Basically, the message is: Stay disciplined, and keep on track. It's easy to let slip one time and then it's even easier to slip further again… and again.

And don't give up – keep at it. People like repetition and familiarity. They want to see you there and they want reinforcement of your message, your needs and your trustworthiness. Besides, it might take time before they see an opportunity to help you.

If times are tough, stay disciplined.

If times are good, stay disciplined.

Find the right referral partners

This is very important. Firstly, it helps to use referral partners who can deliver the goods, and secondly you need to trust them. *And remind me to talk about affiliates.*

OK, let's talk about partners who can deliver the goods. You may get on very well with your friend in the beauty industry, but if you're making and selling bespoke Victorian-style doors, she might not be able to help you... or might she?

Find out. Have 'one-to-ones' with all sorts of business people and friends. A one-to-one is simply a short meeting where two business people exchange information about themselves, their businesses, their objectives and – most importantly – how they can help each other. Start with associates who work in complementary trades. For example, Joe might ask for a one-to-one with an office supplies firm and government-funded business start-up firms. Then start meeting up with the less obvious partners like tree-house builders and canine clothing companies.

By the way, if you don't like or admire someone, maybe don't bother. Remember that you'll need to feel comfortable asking for or receiving a referral from them.

So, how do you do a one-to-one? Firstly, make it clear that's what you want to do, especially if you know that person well: you're going to talk business on that occasion, not catch up with chin-wagging gossip. Agree on an agenda – maybe hand one over and ask if that looks OK to go with. Agree on a time scale.

You need to reciprocate, so make sure you both have a piece of paper to fill in. Here are some things you might like to ask each other:

- Date, location, time (well, you won't need to ask those! I hope).

- Name (yes, yes, you know it, but fill it in before you forget whose details are lurking in your office. Also check you've got the spelling right).

- Contact details, including website(s).

- What does your business offer? (Remember to try to draw out the benefits by asking, 'And that means...?').

- What sort of people / situations have you helped?

- What makes your business better than your competitors? (Again, we're talking benefits.)

- How can I help you?

- What sort of people are you looking for?

- Is there anyone specific you want to meet?

- When do you want to hear from me by?

- Shall we meet again like this? If so, when?

Practise 'active listening' where you listen carefully without trying to guess what they're going to say, and where you aren't planning what you're going to say next. And remember, the point of this exercise is finding out about each other, not pitching for work.

Now file your notes ☺. Before you do, if you've agreed to do anything, get it on your calendar or notice board now!

Ah, thanks for reminding me – affiliates! These are a special type of referral partner, and especially valuable if you have an online business.

The basic principle is that it's good to reward people who have given you a referral, even if it's only a hand-written 'thank you'.

Affiliates are partners you reward with money. Say you want to raise sales of a particular product, but you don't want to spend all your waking hours marketing it across the country. You place an affiliate sign-up on your site. When someone signs up, they get a special code or link. When they send someone to your site via that special link and the visitor buys your product, you pay your referral partner (affiliate) a cut of your profit.

Affiliate commission payments can be automated to make life even easier for you. Commission rates vary from 2% to 60%. Why would you want to pay an affiliate 50% of your profits? Well, why not? Say you do it all by yourself and you sell 100 units at £30 profit each – you get £3000. Say your affiliates bring in an extra 400 sales – that's not only more exposure for your product (always a good thing, I hope), but that's an extra £12,000 – you get £6k and they get £6k … and you've put in very little extra work. Brilliant! Everyone wins.

Why is a 2% rate not such a good idea? Well, unless it's a very high-end product or the lead demands little effort (such as an Amazon link on your site), people won't be motivated to refer to you. So raise the rate and you'll get better returns.

No site? Do it with codes or coupons.

Greet everybody

Simple, really! 'Good morning, I'm Joe Bloggs, of Bloggs' Phones'

Give your tag line or USP

Not sure what I mean? USP means Unique Selling Point, and you can use a tag line to sum it up. Your tag line can be straightforward or maybe a play on words, but the idea is that people will associate the line with you as soon as you name your business.

You need to identify what distinguishes you from your competitors: it could be bigger, better, cheaper... all sorts. If you feel there's nothing singular about your product, then you could differentiate yourself through price, service, innovative feature, guarantee, availability, or by offering bonuses/special offers.

So, in Joe's case for instance, he might offer a much higher-tech phone system than others in his area. He could be offering a free yearly upgrade or a product that's transferable between home and office.

His USP might therefore be that you can carry your phone around with you to use at home or at your place of work without the cost of a mobile/cell phone. To keep bills separate you could, at the touch of a button, switch between 'work' and 'home' modes.

So Joe's tag line might be, 'Phones we can all use anywhere' or 'Phones we can all use anywhere without the cost of traditional mobile phones'. See, it doesn't have to be terribly witty! But say that each time and people will remember it.

What's your USP? How might you encapsulate it? Jot down any ideas now, before you forget them! And if you can't think of a tag line, then ask people to brainstorm it for you ☺.

Start with an attention-grabbing headline

Some people go straight into blah, blah mode, and lose everyone's attention from the outset. Think of several different things to say (one for each occasion), and bring people's attention to it in an ear-catching manner. Use a prop to catch the eye too: a prop helps people remember you, partly because seeing something will reinforce what you tell them but also because you've made an effort. Here are a few openings.

- Who do you know who…?

- Who else wants one of these …?

- Did you know…?

- Finally!

- I nearly didn't get here today…

- One in ten phones…

Look through the headlines of all the adverts you can find, and adapt them for your own needs – your elevator pitch is an advert after all. Here's a list of words you'll often spot in successful adverts.

- Money
- Love
- Guaranteed

- Discovery
- Health
- Safety

- Save
- Proven
- Your family/ loved ones

- Easy
- You
- Protect

- New
- Results
- Free

Of course you can use these words in the body of your message.

Tell a story or say what you do

Or do both. You've grabbed people's attention. Now keep it. The easiest way to do that is to tell a pertinent story or say what you do.

Joe could even paint a picture of the lucrative contract that Jack lost because his phone system wasn't up to 21st century standards and made him look inept.

Brainstorm what you do – in terms of features if you wish. Then work out the benefit(s) for each feature, and then the benefits of the benefits (or 'hidden benefits'). One way to do this is to work through the features and ask yourself what they really mean for the user.

Opposite is an example. You sell the Eezee Computer Chair:

Incidentally, I'm not saying you shouldn't use features, but just keep them for those who want to find out more – or the geeks. In the first instance, hit people's emotions: heart and belly and then brain.

Feature	Which means... benefit	Which means... benefit
Aluminium-steel alloy frame	It's lightweight and strong	Will easily withstand heavy use; easy for you or cleaners to move
Fully adjustable, using simple push-button technology, with 'remember me' function.	It doesn't matter how you're built, you'll be able to easily get the chair to fit your needs.... You can use just one pair per station and keep each shift member happy.	... and not worry about health and safety regulations or about having workers off with bad backs... and anyway, workers will be happy you've invested in them, and happy workers = more productivity / support for you.

Anyway, stop reading now and fill your own product's features and benefits in. A bit stuck? Just jot down all the features and then 'tell' your subconscious to work on it while you carry on. As soon as an idea pops into your head, write it down or take it into a brainstorm.

Another excellent way of working out the benefits to your service or product is to ask your clients and customers – they may even come up with ones you haven't heard of!

You can use the table on the next page to work out some examples. While you're telling your story or explaining what you do, try to use props; they'll help people remember your message more clearly. For example, Joe could stand there and wave around an old-fashioned telephone in one hand and a state-of-the-art one in the other. Or he could pretend to have a phone conversation with someone else in the group (all carefully scripted, of course!).

When you meet up with the same people regularly, there's a danger

Feature	Which means... benefit	Which means... benefit

Further notes / comments / ideas

that you'll assume they know what you're talking about – and also that you'll start using in-jokes. Great fun for the regular group maybe, but it won't get you referrals and it may easily confuse and put off any visitors. Address every audience as if you're speaking to them for the first time.

However, you can involve your audience personally – with powerful effect. Mention their names and people will listen to you. So Joe might say, 'Take Sue, for example: when her client phones for an appointment, what does she want to happen?' You'll have Sue's attention right away! People like to be included, and even if they're not, they like to hear about people they know.

Describe the sort of referrals you are looking for

You can tell the best story in the world, but will that get you referrals? Probably not. Your story might get repeated in the pub and one or two people might be able to see its message, but generally friends and associates need to know what to look out for. It makes it easier for them and they don't risk looking silly either.

Be specific. Saying, 'Who do you know who needs a new phone system?' is better than nothing, but it's a bit vague. I saw one phone system engineer hold up a specific piece of cable. He said, 'Next time you go into an office, look around and see if you can spot cabling that looks like this. If you can, it means their system needs updating. Then please tell me their name and any contact details, and I'll take it from there.' Much better.

You might say you want to know someone who's getting married in the next six months and wants a marquee reception. Or it may be someone who's moving house after July; or who owns a blue

Toyota … whatever. Think who you really want to meet and ask your associates to help you out. You can also say, 'Does anyone here have a contact in the advertising department of Sandy's Superstores? If you do, please would you pass them my name and see if it's OK for me to call them?'

Give your name, business name and tag line

The easy bit again! Joe might say, 'I'm Joe Bloggs of Bloggs' Phones – the phones we can all use anywhere. Good morning.'

Notes on your elevator pitch

- Don't wing your sixty seconds (or whatever slot you've been allocated). It'll show – and you'll have wasted a valuable opportunity to earn a referral. Even if you're going to a conference where you don't know people or what the meeting structure is, have a prepared script that you can whip out with aplomb should the occasion demand.

- Practise out loud at home. What you write down and read in your head may sound great, but it doesn't always translate to the spoken word. Time yourself too, and speak slowly and distinctly. And practise managing your props at the same time.

- If you can talk without reading from a script, that's great, but if you can't, hold it at chest height and look over the top, just glancing down as necessary.

- Watch yourself in the mirror, or get a friend to watch you. Keep your body language open, not closed, and make sure what your body says matches with what your words say. If there's any sort of incongruence, people won't feel confident in you (and they might not even realise why, as it can be very subtle). Without that confidence, they won't give you referrals.

Remember, education is not a dirty word

If you didn't like school, college or university, forget them! Learning is a wonderful thing – and an absolute necessity. You may think you know enough or feel happy as you are. But if you don't keep learning and taking action, then your business won't stand still – it'll fall behind while others overtake you.

Learning is essential to keep your brain active. It opens up opportunities. It brings you into contact with lots of other people. It helps you understand the business world and how people tick. It empowers you to make your business work... and a thousand other things. And yes, it really is fun!

Learning doesn't have to be about taking exams. It can be about going on non-examined courses, signing up for newsletters, attending talks, reading books, listening to CDs... all sorts. Furthermore, if you observe carefully how good teachers teach, you can start to learn more about how to put your message across to other people.
... or why we stop ourselves having a bright future by making decisions **today** based on what has happened to us **in the past**... events which actually have **no relevance** to us today or our future.

Speedboats

Speedboats? Yup; they pop up here and there. In fact, there may be a few ways in which speedboats enter your business life.

1. You're watching them because you're walking by a lake or sea. And you're there because you know exercise gets your brain ticking over very nicely.

2. You're entertaining clients.

3. You're spending some of your well-gotten gains.

4. They're metaphorical speedboats... there – in a sense.

We'll deal with Speedboat Number 4 first. Picture yourself in a speedboat. Really get into it!

- What can you see? ....

....

....

....

....

....

....

....

....

- What can you hear? ....

....

....
....
....
....
....
....
....
....
....
....

- What can you feel? (And what part of your body are you feeling with?)

....
....
....
....
....
....
....
....
....
....
....

Answered those? Good. Now move on to the next page.

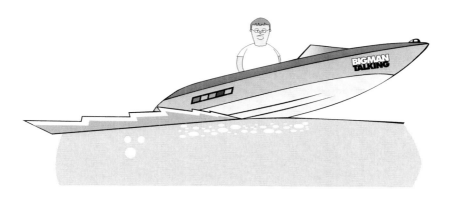

Think back to your answers. See, for example, where the couple in their speedboat are looking. The lady is looking to the side, and the gent to the front (as he's driving, I'm quite pleased about that).

Now, a lot of people tell me things like: *I sat in the boat being driven along, watching the water as it churned up into a beautiful white cascade behind.*

Can you see where I'm going yet? Where you look when you're in a speedboat is a metaphor for what you're doing in your business (and life).

For instance, what's powering the boat? And where is it going? The engine's indirectly powering the boat. The propeller is doing the real work. But all the propeller is doing is leaving turbulence – it has no relevance to direction.

To succeed in business, you need to be able to look around and look to the future. You need to be able to treat the past as just that. It's gone and can't be changed.

Do you have something turbulent from your past (whether it happened two hours ago or twenty years ago) that you keep looking back to and 'watching'? That turbulence could be something major like bankruptcy or divorce, or something smaller like inadvertently upsetting someone. Is it preventing you from looking at what's around you or envisioning the future?

Or are you remembering good, happy things from the past in order to forget what's going on around you, or to take your mind off what might happen tomorrow or next month?

Perhaps you're focusing on the past as a very good way to procrastinate?

To be successful in business it's essential that you spend time looking forward to assess and plan. Failing to plan is like planning to fail.

If you find your past is holding you back, try to identify where you need help.

For example, if you're focusing on happier times in the past because thinking about now and the future just churns your business stomach with apprehension, then here are some options you could choose.

1. Admit it! All business people have things they get stuck on. It's not weak to say so, and it's not weak to ask for help... in fact it shows strength!

2. Identify exactly what help you need. All financial matters, or just your tax returns? All your marketing or specifically your web site and newsletters?

3. Find out who can help you either on a free or low-cost basis (online business forums and training enterprise agencies, for example), or quid pro quo (I'll do your phone calls if you do my tax returns). Or you can opt to pay someone - and if you're

paying it helps to know exactly what you want. If you don't, then pick someone who can help identify your needs.

Maybe some trauma (which may be obvious or hidden) is holding you back. Consider counselling – despite the uninformed stereotypes, it's not 'wet', and it can be very constructive. You can go down the traditional counselling route, or find someone who specialises in NLP (neuro-linguistic programming), hypnotherapy, TFT (Thought Field Therapy), or CBT (Cognitive Behavioural Therapy) for example.

A life coach can help you look at your work-life balance and help you to shift emphasis.

A good business coach can also help you look to the future – more of that in the next section.

If you do go down this route, ask around… and question a therapist before you engage them. Therapists have different characters, and you want one that suits your needs.

If you're being held back by worries or wishing you hadn't done or said something, remember
a) everyone else will have similar stories to tell! What's more,

b) you most likely acted in the way that for whatever reason was *right for you at that time*.

Icebergs, rocks and sunken logs

Networking. I love it! Some people hate it. When I asked some of my clients why, they gave a few different answers. One that's particularly relevant here is, 'I don't know how to do it.'

It's a big, non-specific answer, actually! We'll break it down a bit, into:

- What is networking and what's it for?

- How do I get to go to networking events?

- What do I do when I get there?

- How do I meet people?

- How do I get into conversation with them – and keep it relevant?

- How do I get the most out of it?

- How do I move on to another person or group?

- What do I do after the event?

- Icebergs

- Rocks & sunken logs

In the context of this book, I would define networking as:

Meeting people, finding and talking with ones you can help and the ones who can help you, and arranging a follow-up meeting.

You see, when you network you'll meet many people. You can easily fall at the first hurdle but equally you can make it a big success. Some people you'll meet may be very pleasant, but not what you need. You need to learn to identify quickly who could be a potential customer or supplier, and who could refer you to others.

If you go regularly to a meeting you can take longer to build up your knowledge about individuals, but if you're attending to a one-off conference it helps to know what or who you're looking for. To do that, you must be clear about why you need to network. Not everyone's reasons are the same. Your reason may be very different from your fellow networkers'.

Essentially however, *you are there to build up your business* - more on this soon. You can also learn and share good business practices. Maybe you're there to socialise too, especially if you're a sole trader who works from home.

How do I get to go to networking events?

It's not that difficult to start. Open up your web browser and put in terms such as 'chamber of commerce [your town]'; BNI [your town]; or 'networking groups'. I asked a friend of mine in Bury St Edmunds to do that, as she was new to this scene.

Her search came up with:

-     The Suffolk Chamber of Commerce

-     The Bury St Edmunds Chamber of Commerce

-     Menta and WoMenta

-     The 12:30 Lunch Club

-     BNI East Anglia Chapters

-     The Very Early Lunch Club

… and several more.

The next step is to call or email, ask for details of the next meeting, and see if you can go along.

Another good way is to join business forums (check out relevant ones for you on Google) and attend their local events.

And of course, you can sign up to go to business conferences (sometimes one day long, sometimes more) including those out of your area.

Awards events are also good to get along to – and if you get put up for an award (or put yourself forward), you'll get even more exposure. Find out where awards events are taking place through local business groups, papers and magazines, internet searches and Awards Finder.

What do I do when I get there?

This depends on who you want to meet. Make sure you know who that is! One good way to do this is to identify your current best clients (and if you don't yet have clients, just fantasise!). Are they clients for whom you enjoy really making a difference? Those who pay you lots of money for large jobs – or maybe less money but with repeat orders? Or maybe it's ones who are easy to attract, or those who happily recommend you to others.

Sometimes it's easier to work out who isn't a good client and identify what or who you really don't want in the future. These might be people who are easy to get on with, but you spend a lot of time with them for little financial return. Perhaps they're awkward, so you feel stressed when you think about them. Or maybe you get no repeat business and you find the constant marketing too time-consuming.

It's also good to meet people who can help out your own clients. By bringing the two sets of people together they'll have gained new contacts or clients and they'll feel good towards you. But make sure you check someone out before you refer them.

Another great group of people are those you hit it off with even if they don't want your service… but are very happy to promote you to other people. Make sure you make these people feel appreciated: recompense them with a financial reward, a freebie, or at the very least a handwritten 'thank you' note.

So – you've identified the sort of person you want to meet. This makes life much easier. Even if you find yourself chatting to someone who isn't a likely customer (though see the 'icebergs' bit below), you can ask if they have a contact or know anyone in the room who fits your criteria.

Focusing on what you want makes it happen (look up 'The Law of Attraction' in your library, book shop and the internet). It keeps you in tune so you hear and see what's relevant to you. It also makes you practise more – and practice definitely helps.

But first, you need to approach people. At most networking meetings someone at the door meets, greets and signs you in. Some will have 'runners' who can then introduce you to someone else and get the ball rolling.

Usually, there will be a drink, and sometimes something to eat, so help yourself to refreshments. Make sure you have easy access to your business cards and a pen, so you're not fumbling with a cup or plate.

If there is a runner, ask to be introduced to someone in particular (study the list of attendees before the meeting if one's supplied) or someone who's in a trade that's of interest to you.

But let's assume no-one has approached you or taken you to meet someone. Drink in hand, mouthful finished, pen and cards where you can reach them, look around you. Say there's a room of 30 people. If you're new to all this, it can look a bit daunting. Fear not – there will be plenty of other daunted people in the room!

Many will be hoping for someone to approach them. Some will look plain scared. And some love it - or at least know plenty of people there that they can chat to. (By the way, knowing lots of people cuts both ways: it's easy to get talking – but it can take effort to break away and meet new people if you haven't made a conscious plan to do so.)

Just stand and take in the scene for a minute or so. Identify people who are standing by themselves. That's easy. Now carry on looking,

or just cut straight to the chase and approach one of them. If there's no-one alone, or no-one you feel like approaching, look at the groups of people. Are they standing in a 'closed' formation with bodies, faces and feet facing each other? If they are, and you don't know them well, it's best not to try to butt in, as you'll find it quite difficult. Their body language is saying to others, 'We're having a conversation and we don't particularly want you to join in.'
A few minutes later and the situation may have changed, but in the meantime look for groups of people that are 'open'. Their bodies will be at an angle to each other, and sometimes there's a person-sized space left, indicating it's OK for others to come and join in.

As you approach, ask if you may join them. If they're mid-sentence, gesture with eyebrows and hands rather than butting in verbally.

How do I get into conversation with them – and keep it relevant?

Before I go on here, it's worth pointing out that you'll be more relaxed if you know you don't need to close on a deal in the meeting. Just use the event to enjoy yourself, build up your network, and to arrange a couple of meetings (preferably within the following week) with people you'd like to work with.

If the group of people you've joined turns to you, offer a handshake and introduce yourself. If they're chatting, just add something interesting or helpful at an appropriate juncture, addressing them all at once. Then smile (if you're not doing so already) and introduce yourself.

There are various things you can start with:

• What brought you to the meeting?

• It's my first time to this event. Is it yours?

• Hi, I'm Joe. What trade are you in?

• Mmm, nice food!

• That's an interesting brooch; where did you get it?

• Hi, I'm new here. What's the usual procedure?

• Hey, great talk, wasn't it?

move quickly onto some real questions!

If you're uncomfortable about chatting to strangers, the best thing is to ask them about themselves – and listen to their answers! Don't forget, they may feel awkward to, so you may be doing them a favour! Letting your eyes glaze, butting in, preparing your riposte, or looking over their shoulders is a no-no. Nodding, smiling, asking for detail, and asking the others there how they find networking is fine.

Ask for their business card – two in fact. That way you have one spare to give out and one to keep. Usually, people will ask for yours too. It's OK now to ask, 'How can I help you?' or offer a bit of free and unpatronising advice .

If you're not sure what to ask people, use the 'who-what' approach. Here are a few examples, but start making your own list now.

Who do you...   (work for, want to meet, etc)?

What do you...   (want from X, enjoy, struggle with, etc)?

Why are you...   (at this meeting, needing X, using that, etc)?

Where do you...   (operate from, look for business)?

When do you...   (think you will want to meet, start up, etc)?

How do you...   (manage with X, get to Y, train your team, etc)?

And also, 'I'm interested...' (in hearing more, why you asked that, etc)

It helps to know in advance that you'd like to seek out particular people, professions or trades. Think what you want to ask, and write your questions below.

- **People I want to meet** (note down specific people or a category and status. eg Joel Bloom or A widget company – preferably their advertising manager.)

  ....

  ....

  ....

  ....

  ....

- **Things I want to know and specific questions I should ask**

  ....

  ....

  ....

  ....

It's also good to ask what sort of people they want to meet. In fact, it's often easiest to get on if you go into a networking meeting with the mind that you'd like to help others rather than thinking primarily about what you can get out of it. You can say:

'Oh, Leslie from ABC graphics does that. Would you like me to introduce you?'

'Ah, I know a firm who would help you with that. Would you like their details? In fact, would it help if I tell them about you and ask them to ring you?'

'Hmm. I don't know anyone myself who can help, but I know someone who will. I'll get back to you on that.'

Next, ask for their business card, and jot down on the back what you've promised to do. And do it as soon as possible. Even if you can't help, email to let them know, and say you'll keep an ear out.

How do I get the most out of it?

Make sure you talk to several people, but don't stretch yourself too thin. By the same token, don't just stick to chatting with the first friendly person you meet! They might avoid you in the future, and even if you get on really well it won't have done either of you any favours. Arrange for a meeting later in the week.

Make sure you're wearing a name badge. Place it near to your right lapel (easy for people to see when they shake your hand) and make certain that your name shows clearly, especially your first name (leave out your last name if you prefer).

It can help to put what you do just underneath your name, even if you've been handed a pre-printed badge with your business name on it. AB Supplies doesn't say much, but 'Office Supplies - Same Day Delivery' does. If you have a smart ID badge of your own, don't be afraid to wear it instead of the one you're given at the meeting.

It's pretty important to have business cards, or at least a flyer (home-printed if necessary) showing your details and an outline of what you offer. As well as your name, business name and phone number you should include your tag line, email address and maybe your web address and postal address. (By the way, I've found that assuming people will contact my email address via my website is a mistake!). If your card looks crowded, use both sides. You can also include a few bullet points showing what you do.

The next three tools are also very important … yet they're overlooked or ignored by many! They are your hazelnut, walnut and coconut speeches. Use hazelnuts – small nuggets of information – when people ask you what you do. Use walnuts when they ask you to explain further but you've only got a short time (10-30 seconds) in which to say it. Use coconuts when you can elucidate for a minute or two. Prepare at least three versions of each, practise them out loud, and learn them.

Hazelnuts

Your hazelnut 'speech' is what you do – plus a key benefit. 'I'm in accounting' or 'I am an accountant' just won't do. It's a conversation stopper – not because you're an accountant, but because people have preconceived ideas about what different professions do. So add a powerful benefit: here are some examples.

- Accountant: I help people save at least £5,000 in taxes each year.

- Copywriter: I get you noticed by the people you want to notice you.
- IT consultant: I take away your computer hassles and headaches.

Now, you can create plenty of hazelnuts about any business – just have a handful available and use the one that illustrates what you want to promote on that occasion. It's straightforward enough, but can take some thinking out. Brainstorm (with others if you can). Take any features you come up with (if you're a pilates instructor, for instance, you might take the feature, 'I help people strengthen their pelvic floor muscles'), and instead speak of its benefits ('I stop post-natal incontinence').

Walnuts

When someone hears your hazelnut, they might say, 'Oh, how's that?' or, 'Do tell me more.' If several people in the group want their chance to speak, or you're on your way into a seminar, or in any other situation where you need to be brief, use your walnut. Have the appropriate walnut at the ready to flag what you want to promote that day and again, talk about the benefits that product or service brings.

Your walnut can be a few sentences long, and might include an example. Here's one for starters.
'Have you been in a café where you're distracted – and perhaps disgusted – by flies buzzing around you and your food? Well, I can eradicate flies and ants from food areas. That keeps customers – and health inspectors – happy!'

Coconuts

Your coconut is your 1-2 minute speech. It's more often used for structured meetings such as BNI, where you have the opportunity to stand up and talk about your business for a set period of time.

Use the minute to state your name, business name, possibly your website, the location you work in, who you've helped/how you can help people, and what clients or customers you're looking for. You can start the coconut with your hazelnut or a controversial statement.

Use your nuts

Use your nuts instead of lugging around your business literature. Use your literature for more detailed meetings, post them out or offer them as downloads on your website. Nuts save you juggling and fumbling with papers and can prevent you from appearing either evangelical or desperate!

Let's recap. Listen to others, see if you can help and make appointments to see those that could matter to you in one way or another.

How do I move on to another person or group?

If you're not used to networking, it can be difficult to extricate yourself from a conversation with a particular individual.

In fact, some folks are surprised to find it's generally easier to move away from a group. You gradually stop contributing and while the others are still talking, simply mutter something like, 'Good to meet you', 'Catch you later', and sidle off politely but firmly. Alternatively you might say, 'Let me introduce you to...' and take one of them off to be introduced, or gently grab a passer-by who would interest them, introduce them, and carry on walking to the next group.

Alternatively, ask the group if anyone of them can introduce you to a particular professional or tradesman with whom you'd like to speak. Breaking up is hard to do... Leaving a group when you're enjoying yourself with them or when you fear the next step of connecting with a new set of people can be tough.

Leaving an individual can be tricky too. Maybe:

- the person's even shyer than you and you feel guilty about leaving them.

- the person you're talking to won't take the hint.

- you're genuinely enjoying the conversation.

- you don't want to step outside your new-found comfort zone.

- you don't know how to close your conversation.

It helps to keep your objectives for the meeting in mind: don't go home and dwell on lost opportunities. When there's a slight pause, say, 'It was good to meet you', shake hands, smile and move off.

A bit nervous about doing that? Then thank the person and say something like, 'Shall we go and join that group?' That way, you don't feel bad about leaving them. You can then slide off at an appropriate time – or stick for a while with the new group.

Try asking the person who they most need to meet (like a graphic designer or solicitor, or a specific person), and then say, 'Come with me and I'll introduce you', or, 'Mm, I don't know a solicitor – let's go and ask that group if they do'.

Or you might ask the person if they could introduce you to someone in the IT trade (or whatever). Make clear, 'moving-on' gestures at the same time or you'll give the impression that later will do.
Consider pulling in a passer-by, introducing him or her to the person you want to leave, and bowing out with a gracious smile. Don't feel bad: they may benefit from the meeting, and anyway, they're grown up and capable of handling their own affairs.

By the same token, don't be the person who's impossible to leave! And definitely avoid pinning him or her into a corner and droning on about when you set up, and what you can sell them. That way, disaster lies.

What do I do after the event?

Follow up! Phone, write or email to thank the organisers and stay in touch with interesting new contacts. Make arrangements to meet up if necessary.

And if you have arranged to meet someone, email or phone them to confirm. When you meet up, try to keep to an agenda (maybe a formal one, maybe one in your head), and avoid the temptation to indulge in general chitchat: keep that for another time.

Icebergs

Don't spread yourself too thinly. Most people only ever see the tip of the iceberg. They network hard and continually look for new prospects and people to meet, forgetting that they have actually met enough to get on with and deal with properly. I like to think of this as the 'iceberg theory', which was taught to me by my good friend John Meyer, the USA Co-National Director of BNI.

In essence, what John says is:

'When you see someone at a networking event or anywhere else you may be introduced to people start thinking about what's under the waterline.

When you see an iceberg, you only see the tip of the iceberg above the water - this is the same with the person you just met. Start thinking: who do they know, what groups and clubs do they belong to; where do they live; what did they do before the occupation they have now; and who are their suppliers, clients, and associates?

The list is endless, so who cares if we do business with them? Our role is to make them feel confident in us so they'll pass on our details to people who'll want to use us.'

You can see John's concept illustrated on the next page.

Rocks & sunken logs

Remember the speedboat? That feel of the wind blowing across your face and through your hair, sunshine on face…it's all lovely! But, but, but…

Looking behind and around you is oh so easy to do. You might look behind you because you're hanging on to thoughts of a job or meeting well done, or of something you messed up and you can't forget it.

You may be looking around because you're enjoying the status quo, or because for some reason you don't want to look to the future or because you're avoiding something that's behind you.

In moderation, looking back and looking around aren't problematic, but if you don't keep a close eye on what's in front you'll hit the sunken rock or log in your path. At best it could have you listing badly and at worst, you'll sink without trace.

Some people plan by the seat of their pants and 'cross a bridge when they get to it', but in business that's not always a good strategy. Don't get me wrong – I do believe an ability to think on your feet and react well to unexpected happenings is a great asset.

Sometimes, when I've commented on how successful some people are in business because of their networking and referral skills, people have replied, 'Oh they're just lucky'. No, they're not just lucky. They make their luck. Successful networkers plan ahead the meetings they would like to go to. They'll plan who they'd like to meet or identify the types of contacts they're looking for. They'll plan what they want to ask people and what they want to say about themselves.

In contrast, 'unlucky' people can vaguely hope that they'll get wind of an upcoming meeting. Often however, this strategy won't leave enough time for planning if the meeting or conference isn't local or takes up a few days. They'll trundle along without business details and be unsure who they want to speak to. Some will present their businesses without planning or practising what they want to say. They think they do well 'winging it'. Believe me, they don't. They sound unprofessional – and boring – and leave their listeners in considerable doubt about what they really want.

So, hidden rocks and logs can come in several forms:

- people who don't act on your behalf (even if they really like you) because they don't know what you want.

- getting a referral that you can't carry out because you weren't clear about your business (thereby embarrassing the person who made the referral because he thought you could do it).

- opportunities missed because you don't hear what's going on and fail to look to the future.

- being stitched up because you're unaware of the competition (I personally believe in working with my competitors, not against them – but some people don't feel happy doing that).

- running out of work because you had plenty and neglected to think about work for the future.

- wasting good networking time because you've stuck with just a couple of people.

And of course there are many more. Each person's path is different. Can you think of any rocks or sunken logs you've hit before?

Write them here, and note down how you would avoid them next time.

....
....
....
....
....
....
....
....
....
....
....
....

Referrals

Here are some great ways to get business. The downside is, they're not always targeted, might lead nowhere and can be expensive, time-consuming and scary! They are:

- brochures

- news releases (all media)

- direct mail

- articles (offline and online)

- cold calling

- advertising (in various forms).

But referrals... that's a different story! Referrals are the cream on the cake ☺☺☺

Referrals are generally associated with very little hassle and they're fantastic for increasing your business.

Here are some marketing success statistics.

- Say you send out 1000 mailshot letters (also known as direct mail or junk mail). It's best to buy a targeted list (from a list broker) or use your own client list. From this mailing, 10-20 people will typically sign up to your service or buy your product. In other words, you can expect a response rate of below 2%.

- An enquiry from someone who's been referred to you typically gives an 80% success rate – and with little cost and effort on your part.

People who are referred to you from someone they trust or respect, will already feel well-disposed towards you – and that's a state of mind you can't buy!

If you're in a forum or at a meeting and you explain that you need more information on something, there's usually someone who'll say, 'Hey, see this site! It's got everything you want. And there's more on site B and C too.'

Likewise, if you say you need a widget or service and ask if anyone can help you, you'll get 'Yes, try Boris; he's the man! Here are his details. I know he does his work well; he's not the cheapest but you can be confident it won't fall apart and the job will be done on time. Just mention my name when you contact him. In fact, shall I contact him and ask him to call you?'

In fact, because your contact has even included a 'negative' ('not the cheapest') it makes Boris and his offer seem more realistic. Plus your contact has added that despite the cost he'd use Boris because of his workmanship, so you're already halfway convinced even before you've met Boris. Even if you don't use him in the end, you may well still recommend him to others.

Now, if someone described you with the following words, wouldn't you be happy?

- Conscientious.

- Honourable.

- Gives good guarantees.

- Excellent value for money.

- Gets results.

- Good to work with.

- Explains things well.

- Finishes on time.

These are exactly the kind of words that referrers use about a business they know and trust.

However, I must make this clear right now – referrals do require some work on your part!

1. You have to be clear what sort of clients you're looking for.

2. You must find willing people to recommend you to others.

3. You must follow up with the new prospect.

4. You must reward the person who gives the referral.

5. You must give feedback to the referrer.

We'll look at each of these in more details now.

Be clear about what sort of clients you're looking for

Imagine you're a personal trainer. You can tell me you want contacts from 'people who want to get fit'. Mmm, that's a bit difficult. I know lots of people who want to get fit, but who do you really want to speak to? Is it:

Jason –	he wants to run the London Marathon next year.
John –	he wants to cycle across the Pyrenees in the autumn.
Sahib –	he wants to get up the stairs without puffing.
Sian –	after having three children she's keen to get fit.
Jeni –	she wants to be able to walk a mile now she's recovering from her car accident.

Maybe none of those people are just what you want? I can't say. And I don't know if you'll visit them or expect them to come to you. I don't know the towns and villages in which you operate. I don't know how much you charge, and how often people should attend your sessions.

If you say: I want mothers who are finding it hard to get fit, and maybe feel put off at the thought of joining a gym. They probably feel they're wobbly in the wrong places, have lost some of their strength and balance, their clothes don't fit, they get puffed out easily, and have a poor self-image. Or they may just want to get out and be viewed as a person in their own right rather than someone's mummy. Their babies are old enough to be left with a child minder (I don't have crèche facilities). The mums need to have at least a couple of hours free a week and it will cost them £35 a session.

That's much closer! And you can get even more detailed if you want.

If you then added stories of how you've helped some mums, showed some 'before' and 'after' pictures and testimonials and maybe a video of you in action, then that would really help. If you get a chance, you might even take some of us through a couple of your shorter diagnostic procedures and show us how our posture needs improving (and the knock-on effects and implications) or how we're not quite breathing correctly during exercise.

That'll help us to understand even more clearly what referrals you want. We'll be able to explain to friends and colleagues just what it is you're offering and how well you know your job.

Now, perhaps you want a wider range of clients as well as mums. If so, you'll have to be just as clear about their profiles. When you're trying to deliver the message in a hazelnut, a walnut or even a coconut, it's best to focus on just one client category at a time. If you get to speak for 10-20 minutes, perhaps you could cover three.

One more thing here – it helps to explain who you don't want as well. If you've asked for people who want to get fit and I send John (the would-be Pyrenees cyclist) to you but you have no idea about cycling, or no interest in the issues it creates, or the wrong facilities, then you will look silly, John will be annoyed, and I will feel peeved.

Be clear. Be specific. It works.

Have willing people to help you out

This is really useful! There are groups of people who are more likely to help you such as:

- ✓ Those who have used and benefitted from your product or service.

- ✓ Those you've helped (either with advice or referrals).

- ✓ Folks you ask in such a way that they'd be pleased and proud to help you.

- ✓ Those who know exactly what or who you're looking for.

- ✓ People with a wide circle of friends, family, acquaintances and associates.

- ✓ Those you reward in a way which makes them feel good.

Remember, in the words of Ivan Misner (the man who founded the BNI referrals business), 'Givers gain'. It means that if you help others, they'll want to help you.

Now, it could be that the people in your group genuinely don't know any good business contacts for you... but remember the iceberg! I know lots of people: some are mums and some are married to mums, and some are single and fit young men. They in turn will know more people, and so on. Start the ball rolling.

Follow up with your new prospect

As soon as you've been given details of a new prospect, or as soon as the prospect contacts you, follow them up. Find out what they need and want at an early stage, so if you aren't the right person you can stop before anyone gets annoyed or offended. And if you know someone who can help the prospect instead of you, offer their details. They'll think you're great – and what could have been a negative becomes a positive.

Don't leave it a few days before you establish contact, as that will reflect badly on you and the referrer. If you're going to be out of the office, leave a message on your answer phone and set up an email autoresponder message. Say when you'll return and that if they leave their details you'll contact them as soon as possible after you get back.

Reward the person who makes the referral

Ignore this bit at your peril! If you don't thank people in an appropriate way, you'll come across as ill-mannered, ignorant, selfish and as someone who doesn't value others' contributions. I know an accountant who regularly referred people to a solicitor. He told me one day he was going to stop doing it.

'Why's that?' I asked. He replied that the solicitor had made a lot of money through these referrals. My accountant friend wasn't complaining about the solicitor making money. The problem was, he never said thank you and not once did he reciprocate. I'm afraid to say, the solicitor was in the same BNI chapter as the accountant, and should have known better.

Sometimes a referral doesn't end up in more sales for you, but you can still thank your referrer for trying. Here are some good ways to reward your referrers:

- a public thank you, maybe with a card, flowers, chocolates, wine or other thoughtful gift.

- a larger gift (sometimes perceived as more valuable than a cash equivalent).

- a 'thank you' card or letter in the post.

- an obvious, ongoing attempt to reciprocate by finding referrals for your referrer.

- a one-off cash incentive (eg. 10% of the first job from your new client).

- a recurring incentive (for example, if someone joins your membership site through your referrer's efforts, then offer them a cash payment for as long as the member stays with you).

Affiliate schemes are the online version of referral fees. They're pretty easy and cheap to set up thanks to new software packages. A good affiliate system can be automated, so there's little effort on your part to make sure your monthly 'thank you' fees go out.

Properly thanked, your contacts are far more likely to try to find you more referrals. What's more, others will notice your efforts and feel good about you too – which in turn may lead to more referrals.

Give follow-up news to the referrer

Sorry, there will be a lot of the words 'referral' and 'referrer' in this section – no way around it. Anyway, it's not only polite to thank a referrer for their efforts, but it also pays to give follow-up news. This can work in two ways.

The first is that if the referrer got the wrong end of the stick, it's now time to come clean. That way, any potential awkwardness between any of the parties involved can be neatly nipped in the bud. It's important to sort out any misunderstandings quickly and in a friendly fashion. Also ask each other how you may help in another way.

The second way of giving follow-up feedback is this: when you tell your referrer exactly how you were able to help and the benefits you delivered to the person they referred, then that referrer has learned even more about your business and what makes a great referral for you. This means their next referrals will be even better targeted. And of course, the referrer will be pleased you've taken the time to feedback what happened as a result of their efforts.

Even better, they'll know that the person they referred you to will be feeling good about them: brownie points all round!

Why's words (Sorry!)

This final section aims to wrap up all that has gone before with four handy prompts to keep you on track as you head off for networking and referral success.

1. Why...

For your network to be able to recommend you, they'll need to know why **you** do what you do. What's in it for you? Most people are motivated by more than just money – and it's those passions and energies that make your business attractive and special. In my case, two dear friends had died without ever having prepared for such an eventuality: in both cases, their families were left in financial ruin. I keenly wanted to prevent that happening to others, so I spend my life doing all I can to help people strengthen and safeguard their lives and interests.

2. Why...

So you've put together your Top Ten list of 'most wanted' referrals? Great. But **why** do you want them? Do your network colleagues know? If not, be sure to teach them well. The more they understand about why Sir Richard Branson is a great referral for you, the more they'll learn about who else could be good for you too.

3. Why...

It's that Top Ten list again. **Why** would they want to speak to you? What could you do for them that others wouldn't fulfil? Imagine that you have a business proposition you'd like to put to Sir Richard Branson and I have that contact for you. I'd need to feel very confident about why Sir Richard would want to speak to you rather than another supplier. After all, there's no way I'd be prepared to upset my relationship with Sir Richard – or indeed any of my contacts. If I don't know why it's a good idea for them to talk to you then I wouldn't make the introduction.

4. Price *(Well, I had to ring the changes somewhere!)*.

Last but definitely not least – price can be a real barrier, and not always in the way you'd expect. The price you quote has to be right for the customer. 'Of course', you say. But your customers will not all share the same attitude to price. If you're selling your up-to-the-minute database system to a small and growing business they might be willing to pay you £2000 for your work. On the other hand, try selling that same database at the same price to a major high street brand, and they'll ignore you completely. They'll be expecting to pay many thousands for their system – and they'll not entertain low-cost suppliers whose prices might indicate a low-quality system. No matter how brilliant your database system might be, they'll simply never know! So be clear about your pricing policy and if you want to approach different markets, be prepared to price differently too.

And of course, make sure your referral partners know and understand your policy and practice. It matters – and so do they.

Life, Business & Speedboats

Life, Business & Speedboats

Life, Business & Speedboats